The Christmas Caper

And Other Christmas Dramas

Rod Tkach

CSS Publishing Company, Inc.
Lima, Ohio

FIRST EDITION
Copyright © 2023
by CSS Publishing Co., Inc.

Library of Congress Cataloging-in-Publication Data:

Names: Tkach, Rod, author.
Title: The christmas caper : and other Christmas dramas / by Rod Tkach.
Other titles: Christmas caper (Compilation)
Description: Lima, Ohio : CSS Publishing Company, Inc., 2023.
Identifiers: LCCN 2023032517 (print) | LCCN 2023032518 (ebook) | ISBN
   9780788030949 (paperback) | ISBN 9780788030956 (adobe pdf)
Subjects: LCGFT: Christmas plays. | Drama.
Classification: LCC PS3620.K33 C48 2023 (print) | LCC PS3620.K33 (ebook)
   | DDC 812/.6--dc23/eng/20230718
LC record available at https://lccn.loc.gov/2023032517
LC ebook record available at https://lccn.loc.gov/2023032518

For more information about CSS Publishing Company resources, visit our website at www.csspub.com, email us at csr@csspub.com, or call (800) 241-4056.

e-book:
ISBN-13: 978-0-7880-3095-6
ISBN-10: 0-7880-3095-7

ISBN-13: 978-0-7880-3094-9
ISBN-10: 0-7880-3094-9

PRINTED IN USA

Table of Contents

The Christmas Caper

Narrator 1: Christmas has been reported missing! Some famous detectives have been called in to help solve the case. Here they are dunkin' their donuts in their hot chocolates. *(pictures at donut shop; cast with donuts and hot chocolate; individual shots and around the table)*

Narrator 2: *Jessica Far-Fetcher* came in from Cabot Cove, Maine. She has a habit of meddling in other people's cases. She saw a posting about this case on social media. When it comes to solving a mystery Jessica believes two things are absolutely necessary: shrewd observation and unabashed nosiness. Jessica can be a pest that not even Terminix can control!

Narrator 1: When Commissioner Kliferd of the NYPD told Marshall Sam McShroud about the case, McShroud immediately saddled up leaving behind city sidewalks, busy sidewalks, dressed in holiday style. Silver bells, the TSA lines swell, it's not easy flying out of the city!

Narrator 2: The famous detective from 221B Baker Street in London has thrown his hat into the ring. A bit out of his element, *Sherlock Homes* won't have the luxury of the "Baker Street Irregulars;" his group of street children who serve as informants.

Nor does he have his sidekick Dr. Watson. We will see if the science of deduction holds on both sides of the pond.

Narrator 1: Christmas is one of the world's greatest treasures. When it comes to treasure hunters, **Indiana Bones** is in a class all by himself. When it comes to antiquities, who would know more than a college archaeology professor like Indy? Is anyone surprised that he left the library to join this group of detectives? After all, he once told his students, "If you want to be a good archaeologist, you *gotta* get out of the library!"

Narrator 2: The **Red Beret Girls** are in middle school at St. Veronica's, an all-girls school on New York's upper east side. Being from Manhattan is revealing in itself. Sophie and Margaret are great friends whose lives revolve around their studies, their hobbies, and being sleuths in school uniforms. They have an easier time solving mysteries than they do solving the mystery of boys.

Narrator 1: The youngest detective in this group is none other than **Cam Hansen**. Cam is an elementary student… didn't Homes say it was elementary? Her friends say she has a mental camera. It's as if she has photographs stored in her head. When she wants to remember something, she takes a good look, blinks her eyes, and says, *"Click!"*

Narrator 2:	Let's listen in on their conversation.
Far-Fetcher:	"There are three things you can never have enough of in life: chocolate, friends, and the theater."
McShroud:	"I get chocolate and friends. But when I am in the theater, I feel like a bull in a prize flower bed."
Cam:	(looks at McShroud) *"Click!"*
McShroud:	"What did she do that for?"
Homes:	It just might be that our first clue is more than we could barter for! It's off to the theater!
Narrator 1:	Christmas is missing and they're off to the theater? Are they expecting a Miracle on 34th Street? *(pictures outside of theater)*
Far-Fetcher:	"I don't want to alarm you but something sinister is going on here."
Sophie:	"It's a dickens of a tale: Christmas is missing."
Margaret:	"Do we have a ghost of a chance of solving this?"
Narrator 2:	Indy finds a ticket stub. Clearly the show is over. The ticket says they were off base in their first try of solving this mystery.
Homes:	There are signs of Christmas, but Christmas is still missing. We must get back in the game.

McShroud:	"Where I come from, when we get on the trail of something, we just mount up and ride off." *(pictures getting into cars/ arriving at store that has sporting goods, toys, books; such as Walmart, etc.)*
Narrator 1:	Here we see Indy trying to catch a clue. *(picture by fishing stuff)*
Homes:	Nice try Indy but that's not the clue we need.
Sophie:	I found pieces to the puzzle…boxes of them! *(picture w/ puzzles)*
Margaret:	I've got it. Let's leap-frog to another part of the store. There are no clues here. *(picture holding leap-frog)*
Narrator 2:	There's a song in the air. Maybe there's a clue there.
Cam:	(Looking at detectives with Christmas CD's) *"Click"*
Far-Fetcher:	"Here Comes Santa Claus" and "Grandma Got Run Over by a Reindeer" don't get us any closer to solving the case.
Margaret:	What about a Blue Christmas?
McShroud:	Nothing will get as lonesome as a New Mexico beaver. But if we don't find Christmas, I will have to rethink that!
Homes:	We've seen signs of Christmas, but Christmas is still missing. When you have eliminated the impossible, whatever remains, must be the truth.

| **Indy:** | Did you get that out of a book of quotes? Maybe there is a clue in store for us. |

Indy: Did you get that out of a book of quotes? Maybe there is a clue in store for us.

Narrator 1: Here we see our detectives at work in a book store. *(pictures of detectives checking place out)* It seems that one book has captured their attention. Could *"How the Grinch Stole Christmas"* be a clue? Is that why Indy is pointing to the book? *(picture of Indy pointing at book)*

Far-Fetcher: There's just something that doesn't seem right.

Sophie: There are no clues to build on.

Indy: Let's do it.

Sophie: Do what?

Homes: It's elementary. We go to a place that builds. Maybe we can find something to build upon. *(pictures of Home Depot type place and detectives)*

Narrator 2: Could this be the time and place: to see if the detectives could get squared away? If the clues would measure up? If the case could be cut down to size? *(pictures of detectives by the tools)*

Cam: *"Click!"*

Homes: These clues are washed out. They might as well be hung out to dry. *(pictures by washers/dryers)*

Cam: *"Click!"*

McShroud:	This is the berries! Finding no clues is like having Christmas without candy canes or Christmas cookies. *(pictures at grocery store by cookies)*
Far-Fetcher:	This just isn't adding up. The lack of clues has left us up a creek without a paddle. *(pictures at sporting goods store by kayaks, canoes)*
Narrator 1:	Maybe a stop by the electronics will help. There's a possibility of making connections that have been beyond our Verizon.
Narrator 2:	The detectives sprint to the phones. Unfortunately, the number they needed was no longer in service. *(pictures by phones; pictures with detective on phone)*
Cam:	*"Click!"*
Narrator 1:	Christmas creativity happens with decorations. Maybe these detectives will find clues of Christmas among trees and flowers, or ornaments and stockings. *(pictures in of detectives in these sections)*
Cam:	*Click!"*
McShroud:	When the hound is chasin' the rabbits, the fox has the run of the woods. We've been chasin' clues, but Christmas is still missing!
Sophie:	We need a break.
Margaret:	Today?
Homes:	Yes, the arches. I'm lovin it.

Narrator 2:	Mickey D's brought new inspiration as the snack fueled their determination to solve the Christmas Caper. Cam took a few more mental pictures.

Cam: *"Click!"*

Sophie: You've taken a lot of pictures Cam. Your camera card must be full.

Margaret: All those pictures. Did we learn anything?

Narrator 1:   The pictures provided evidence of Christmas but not Christmas itself. Christmas was still missing even though the detectives ran into many people getting ready for Christmas.

Far-Fetcher: The signs of Christmas are everywhere, but Christmas is missing.

McShroud: Maybe we need to look at the word Christmas.

Homes: Do you think the word Christmas is a clue?

Cam: *"Click!"*

McShroud: The "m-a-s" or "mas" of Christmas means festival. Put it together… Christmas is Christ's festival.

Far-Fetcher: How can you have a festival of Christ without Christ?

Homes: Indy just handed me a note. It says, "I think it's time to ask yourself, 'What do you believe in?'"

Far-Fetcher:	Indy just handed me a note too. It says, "It's a leap of faith. Maybe we should check the original story. Maybe we aren't the first detectives looking for Christmas."
Cam:	*"Click!"*
McShroud:	There you go. Now you're ridin' a trail that can be followed.
Far-Fetcher:	Check the original source? It's so elementary!
Homes:	Wouldn't that be the gospel of Matthew, chapter one, verses 18-25?
Reader:	*(Reads that scripture)*
Sophie:	The first Christmas detectives....in fact, there they are! *(Wise guys appear at back of the church.)*
Margaret:	They want us to join them!
Sophie:	WAIT! After all those years in Catholic school, I know there's more.
Reader:	*(Reads Matthew 2:1-12)*
Margaret:	Now?
Sophie:	Now! *(Detectives go to the back of the church as organ plays "We Three Kings")* *(Angel carrying the star leads one wise guy down center aisle)* *(Wise guys lead detectives down the aisle to the nativity)*

(While they are going to the back, Mary, Joseph, and manger appear on stage)

(When wise guys & detectives get to the front, they gather around the nativity, Mc-Shroud asks)

McShroud: Hey, Wise Guys, how did you know where to find Christmas?

Wise Guy 1: Followed God's clues

Cam: *"Click"*

Wise Guy 2: Found the good news:

Cam: *"Click"*

Wise Guy 3: Jesus is born!

Cam: *"Click"*

Narrator 2: Got it give it up for those Wise Guys. *(Detectives clap)* They got it right back then and they showed these detectives how it's done old school. Worshiping the Christ is the only way to truly have Christmas. Otherwise, you're just left with a lot of signs. I wonder if people will get the picture?

Cam: *"Click!"*

Homes: Now that Christmas is no longer missing, what are we to do?

McShroud: Back home, we'd go tell it on the mountain. See no reason why it won't work here. *(cast sings refrain and then takes a bow)*

The Gift

Introduction: The Gift is a puppet play that explores the ultimate Christmas gift. The older youth in the church pre-recorded the script thereby allowing their full attention in working the puppets. It is important to anticipate audience reaction when working up the script for recording. Doing so allows the congregation to get the full impact of The Gift.

Caleb:	Wow! Hannah, do you see all those people out there?
Hannah:	I sure do, Caleb. Wonder what they're all doing here?
Caleb:	I wonder: are they real?
Hannah:	Are they what?
Caleb:	Mom, are those people out there real? Or are they a fig-a-mints of the imagination?
Mom:	Figments of the imagination usually don't look so real. Besides, would a figment of the imagination fall asleep in church?
Hannah:	That's about the only way to get by with it, right Dad?
Dad:	Who's getting by with what? And what are all those people doing here? Is this for real or did we step into another matrix?
Hannah:	Another what?
Dad:	A matrix is a mold or form, like your Mom's Jell-O® molds.

Caleb: So it's a place where things take shape?

Dad: Yes, but….

Caleb: But, what's that got to do with this? If those people out there are real, they certainly aren't made of Jell-O®! I don't see any that are grape flavored.

Mom: Our matrix is the little puppet theater. But tonight our matrix is more like Broadway: we've hit the big time!

Caleb: But are all those people out there real?

Hannah: Or are they just puppets, acting or playing parts in our imaginations?

Caleb: Grandpa, you've been around longer than any of us. What do you think?

Grandpa: Oh, they're real all right: at least in the sense that they are breathing and have a pulse!

Grandma: This is serious, dear. The children really want to know.

Hannah: So, are Grandpa and Grandma saying that some people who have a pulse and are breathing aren't real? If they aren't real, what are they?

Caleb: Wouldn't it be a hoot if they were puppets with someone pulling their strings?

Dad: There may be more truth to that than you know.

Hannah: Caleb, (gives Dad the look) Dad's just messin' with you. That can't be right, can it?

Grandma: In a way, yes it is.

Caleb: I'm right! I'm right! (triumphantly) But, I don't have a clue why. (confused)

Mom: The life of a puppet is lived by a script. It tells us where we can go, what we can do, and even what we say.

Dad: But people have a different matrix. They are free to go, do, and say what they want.

Grandpa: Or, at least that's what they think. But, if you go back to the beginning you find out that the very first people, Adam and Eve, sinned.

Grandma: The matrix that God created for them was so awesome: it was especially for them. But they disobeyed God by taking something he said they couldn't have.

Hannah: Boy, we get in trouble when we do that!

Caleb: So, what happened? Did they get "time out?"

Mom: I'll say.

Dad: God's first question wasn't "why did you do it?" It was "where are you?" Because of their sin, they couldn't stay in the garden like God had planned.

Hannah: Sin caused all that?

Grandpa: Sin is very powerful. Their Bible says that people are darkness before they come to know God.

Caleb: You mean, they are in darkness, don't you?

Grandma: No, Grandpa is right. Their whole matrix of living is darkness. They are controlled by selfishness and sin.

Dad: They think they are free; but they aren't.

Hannah: You mean they just play out their roles without realizing it?

Mom: Oh, if you ask them, they'll tell you different. But that's because they don't know that something is very wrong. Or if they do know, they don't want to admit it.

Caleb: So how do they quit playing a role and start being real? They can become a *real person*, right?

Grandpa: Yes, each and every one can become a real person. But it a choice. They have to receive *the gift* if they are going to become real.

Hannah: We like gifts, don't we Caleb?

Caleb: Especially that great big one under the tree with my name on it!

Grandma: This gift isn't under the tree but it is the most important gift of all.

Dad: It's the gift that changes them from darkness to light.

Mom: It's the gift that keeps on giving.

Caleb: Boy, would I like a gift like that! We'd never have to replace the batteries!

Hannah: Just what kind of gift are you talking about?

Mom: A gift that is reflected in your names.

Caleb: What do our names have to do with this?

Dad: The name Caleb means bold, faithful. The name Hannah means grace.

Grandpa: God did something very bold and faithful so people could become real.

Grandma: As an act of grace, God became human and was born as a baby!

Hannah: Why would he do that?

Mom: The only way to change people and the matrix they are caught in was to enter that matrix and break its power.

Dad: For God so loved the world that he gave his only begotten Son that whosoever believes in him should not perish but have eternal life.

Caleb: So *the gift* is God's Son?

Grandpa: Yes!

Hannah: But how does *the gift* help them become *real*?

Grandma: In Christ a person becomes a new creature, the old things have passed away; new things have come.

Mom: It's no longer sin pulling the strings.

Dad: God cuts those strings and makes changes from the inside out.

Grandpa: Jesus shapes a person according to his character.

Grandma: Receiving *the gift* of Jesus begins a process of becoming like him.

Caleb: So the more a person becomes like Jesus, the more real they become?

Hannah:	And the more authentic and genuine they become?
Mom:	That's right!
Caleb:	Of all the gifts at Christmas, this one has to be the most awesome gift of all.
Hannah:	Looking at all the people out there I can't help but wonder, have they received *the gift*?

A Misplaced Christmas

Greeting: Good evening. It is my pleasure to welcome you to our program. Without giving away too much of the story, our program portrays what happens in preparing for a program. A lot of work has gone into this: parents have been faithful in making sure practices were well attended, participants have been faithful in learning their parts, and you are being faithful by being here. Speaking of faithful, let us stand and join together in singing, *"O Come, All Ye Faithful."*

***Christmas Carol:** *"O Come, All Ye Faithful"* Congregation

Narrator A: You may be seated. Imagine you are in a traditional brick church, complete with stained glass windows, a sanctuary with hard wood floors, and a cornerstone that reads 1928. In the 1950s the "new" education addition provided much needed space: a kitchen and fellowship hall in the basement as well as a meeting room and offices on the second floor.

Narrator B: On the third floor there are class rooms and one very, very small and very over stuffed storage area. It didn't matter *what* one was looking for, it was **the** place to look; but good luck trying to find it. Forgetting to duck when exiting through its small door could leave quite a mark! And you best be able to walk sidewise because it's the only way to get past all the stuff!

Narrator A: The writers of unsolved mysteries know the answer before anyone else. The same is true for those who "move" things when a church renovates. Unfortunately, the

program director, Miss Direction, was not in on the reloca-
tion of all the essentials of a Christmas program. Props and
costumes come to mind. Miss Direction is doing her best to
live through the first rehearsal.

Narrator B: And it came to pass that the time to practice the
program did arrive; but would the director, Miss Direction,
survive? That the costumes and props were missing was
clear, not finding things was a cause of great fear.

Miss Direction:	Oh me, Oh my, I feel like little Bo Peep; *(flustered)* for I went to the storage area, and there were no sheep! They have *always* been there for me to see I can't imagine where they could be.
Janitor:	Miss Direction, you look confused.
Miss Direction:	I went to the storage area on the third floor and it's missing.
Janitor:	Missing? I hate to tell you this, but the third floor is just where I left it. It's been there since the place was built.
Miss Direction:	Not the third floor, the storage closet. *(exasperated)*
Janitor:	The storage closet isn't missing, I just came from there. I opened the door, but I don't go where angels fear to tread.

Miss Direction: It's not the closet that's missing, it's the sheep. They're gone! I opened the closet, and the whole flock is gone. I went to where they have always been…and… there's shelves in there. We've never had shelves before. And, get this, the shelves are full of quilting supplies. The only thing I found was the manger. How in the world am I to find white sheep in the midst of boxes of batting?

Janitor: Have you tried calling?

Miss Direction: Whom should I call? I'm sure 9-1-1 would be less than thrilled with an emergency call about missing sheep!

Janitor: Not 9-1-1, but the sheep. Call the sheep…by name. That's what a shepherd does. Jesus compares us to sheep and calls us by name. If it works for a shepherd and works for Jesus, maybe it will work for you. I best be getting back to my job. If I see any wooly critters, I'll send 'em your way. *(exits after lines)*

Miss Direction: Why didn't I think of that? *(calls them by name, however many are in the program… sheep enter when called)* Where have you been? Do you have any idea how worried I have been? What do you have to say for yourselves?

Sheep: Baa, baa, baa

Miss Direction:	Where's the cow? And where's the donkey? We can't have a nativity without the cow and donkey…it just won't look right. I've spent hours looking, it's no good. I'd cry like a baby if I could.
Sheep:	Baa-baa-moo, ba-baa-moo, *(sing it twice) (to Braham's lullaby)*
	baa-baa- moo, baa-baa-moo-baa
	(sheep lay down after)
	baa-baa-hee; baa-baa-haw;
	(singing)
	baa-baa-hee, haw, hee-haw
Miss Direction:	For a critter chorus, you were awesome! Maybe I'll be serenaded by shepherds. But since they've been misplaced, no chance of that happening.
Narrator A:	(Reads Luke 2:1-7)
Narrator B:	(Reads Luke 2:8-11)
Shepherd 1:	Come on guys, I found where our sheep went!
Shepherd 2:	Looks like we wandered smack dab into a Christmas program!
Shepherd 3:	Ah, yes, and the angel said a Savior has been born in the city of David.
Shepherd 4:	And the sign will be a baby wrapped in clothes, lying in a manger.

Miss Direction:	Where have you guys been?
Shepherds:	You talking to us?
Miss Direction:	Do you see any other shepherds? I've searched high and low for you; couldn't find you anywhere. What do you have to say for yourselves?
Shepherd 1:	We've *always* been put away with the manger, except this last time.
Shepherd 2:	We were put away from the manger.
Shepherd 3:	We were separated from our sheep, couldn't hear a peep.
Shepherd 4:	Being back together puts a song in the heart.
Miss Direction:	What a great idea. The shepherds and sheep can sing the first verse of *Away in a Manger* and our song leader will cue the congregation to join in on the second and third verses. *(singing of song)*
Shepherd 1:	Do you know that the multitudes of angels praised God too? *(speaking to Miss Direction)*
Shepherd 2:	They said, "Glory to God in the highest."
Shepherd 3:	"And on earth peace among people with whom God is well pleased."
Shepherd 4:	We heard it with our own ears, saw it with our own eyes. It was something!

Narrator A:	And the shepherds went back, glorifying and praising God for all that they had heard and seen, just as had been told them. *(shepherds sit down)*
Miss Direction:	We've got sheep, the shepherds, the cows, the donkeys. You guys sit in the first pew; I don't want to lose you! If I only had the wise guys.
Three Kings:	We three kings have tele-star *(enter rapping)* our GPS has taken us far; *(hamming it up)* over field and fountain, moor and mountain *(on way to platform)* following heaven's star.

We three kings have been on a trip
our camels came fully equipped.
Ol' King Herod we gave the slip
to worship the Christ was quite hip.

We followed a star of wonder, a star of
light
a star which led us just right
Brought us to that very place
where God was born as truth and grace.

Miss Direction:	Where did you guys come from? I've searched high and low.
King 1:	Did you search way up north?

Miss Direction: Let me see…that would be the bell tower! Goodness gracious, we've never stored anything up there but the Christmas tree. Of course I didn't look there. But you can bet I will next year.

King 1: It won't help. We weren't there.

King 2: Miss Direction, did you search the deep south?

Miss Direction: You bet I did…there was so much stuff under that stairwell that I was tempted to call waste management and have them back up a truck. But who would dare do such a thing? Fortunately, the pastor has refined the area. It's limited to silk poinsettias and the large Christmas wreaths. Why would you be there?

King 2: We didn't say that's where we came from, we just asked if you looked!

King 3: Did you look over the west?

Miss Direction: I was tied in knots trying to find you guys. But what once was the Christmas closet is now a quilter's haven. There's enough material, needles and batting in there to blanket the heavens.

King 3: So you did look?

Miss Direction: You weren't there. So where did you guys come from?

Kings 1, 2, 3: Listen to the Christmas story…it will tell you.

| **Narrator B:** | "...now after Jesus was born in Bethlehem of Judea in the days of Herod the king, behold, Magi from the _east_ arrived in Jerusalem." |

| **Kings 1, 2, 3:** | Get it? We came from the Christmas storage area in the east corner of the building. It's between the junior high room and the handicap bathroom. |

| **Miss Direction:** | I can't help but wonder if this isn't a "once upon a time" story. But you're here now, that's what matters most. Please take your seats. (*Kings sit down*) |

(After they are seated, Carpenter Fred enters with cocky confidence and complete tool belt. As he is walking through Miss Direction has a question)

| **Miss Direction:** | Carpenter Fred, I have a question for you? |

| **Carpenter Fred:** | What's that? |

| **Miss Direction:** | The cornerstone on this building goes back almost one hundred years. Right? |

| **Carpenter Fred:** | That's right...it's been here longer than I have! |

| **Miss Direction:** | My family has been part of this church from the beginning. Not once has there been anything that comes close to being a storage area by the junior high room. Yet, these wise guys say there is. What gives? |

Carpenter Fred: Kings are not the only ones to travel afar. Take me, my hammer and crowbar. We remodeled to say the least. Now there are storage rooms in the east. So the kings really are guys who are wise. Their destination came as a surprise!

Miss Direction: Thanks Carpenter Fred. That clears things up a lot.

Miss Direction: Now where was I? We have the sheep, the shepherds, the donkeys, and the cows. We have the wise guys. We have the manger. I know I'm forgetting something. I feel like I'm doing this on a wing and a prayer.

Carpenter Fred: Maybe it would help if we sang a song. You've got a ready-made choir out there. *(points to congregation)* I'm sure they would sing *Hark! the Herald Sing* if they knew it would help you out. It's found on page _________ of your hymnal.

You guys ready to sing? Let's do it!

Carpenter Fred: My, my....such sweet, sweet music to work by!

Angels: *(angels enter while congregation is singing; take their places around the manger)*

Miss Direction: What angelic voices! What heavenly singing! And my angels are here! How did you get here?

Angel 1: Let me tell you, it was no easy trip.

Angel 2:	First we had to go way upstairs. Do you have any idea how many stairs there are?
Angel 3:	In case you're wondering, angel wings are fitted up there.
Angel 4:	Then we had to trek all the way to the basement. More stairs.
Angel 5:	The halos are stored down there.
Angel 6:	Then it was back up to the main floor because someone moved the wings to the fireside room.
Angel 1:	Up the stairs, down the stairs, up the stairs again…this place has been covered by angels.
Angel 2:	It's a miracle that we're on time.
Miss Direction:	These angels are beautiful! But where did these costumes come from?
Carpenter Fred:	I believe I can answer that. When the old storage area upstairs was renovated, so were the costumes. Actually, they were replaced by the group of ladies that keeps this place in stitches. Any other questions?
Miss Direction:	Carpenter Fred, you have been a God-send. Thank you for your help. If I need you again, I'll be able to find you in the furnace room, right?
Carpenter Fred:	If you don't mind, I think I'll just rest my legs and park it in the pew. I'm curious what these angels might be up to.

| **Narrator B:** | After the angel broke the news about Jesus' birth to the shepherds a whole host of angels burst on the scene. They were all praising God saying, "Glory to God in the highest, and on earth peace among people with whom God is pleased." |

Narrator B: After the angel broke the news about Jesus' birth to the shepherds a whole host of angels burst on the scene. They were all praising God saying, "Glory to God in the highest, and on earth peace among people with whom God is pleased."

Miss Direction: Now that the heavenly host, the angels, are present and accounted for, they can be seated. But it still seems like we are missing something. But what?

Shepherds: *(from where they are sitting)* You're missing Joseph!

Kings: *(from where they are sitting)* You're missing Mary!

Whole Cast: *(from where they are sitting)* And what about Jesus?

Miss Direction: The marvel of Joseph and Mary is that I knew where those costumes were; at least I thought I did. After the program last year, I took them home to clean them. It's a good thing I remembered to bring them back for this dress rehearsal.

Joseph & Mary: *(entering together)*

Joseph: Isn't this supposed to be a dress rehearsal?

Mary: We couldn't find our costumes anywhere!

| **Miss Direction:** | I can't imagine why, I had them at home. If it wasn't for digging out all the Christmas decorations, they would still be there. Here, put them on and then take your places by the manger. *(put on costumes, take places)* |

| **Mary** | Joseph, did you have the baby? |

| **Joseph** | I don't think so! If I remember the story, having the baby is your department. |

| **Miss Direction:** | We have the baby for the manger. *(baby is placed in manger)* We have Joseph and Mary, the shepherds, the sheep and the rest of the critters. We have the wise guys and the angels. Let's get everyone in their places. |

| **Whole Cast** | *(looking into manger and then asking Miss Direction)* What child is this? |

| **Miss Direction:** | I think you know…but just to make sure, we'll let the people out here answer that as the whole congregation sings, *What Child is This* found on page ______. |

| **Miss Direction:** | Wow, this is picture perfect. Be still for a bit as we stop and think about all that God did to make Christmas happen. |

| **Narrator A:** | And the **angels**, after announcing the birth, *returned* to heaven. |

(angels exit)

And the **shepherds** *returned* to their fields after their Bethlehem visit.

(shepherds exit)

And the **Magi** *returned* to their country by a different way.

(Magi/kings exit)

Miss Direction: With all these Christmas returns, what about Joseph, Mary, and Jesus?

(speaking to herself)

Narrator B God warned Joseph in a dream and they left for Egypt.

(Joseph, Mary, and Jesus exit)

Miss Direction: Now that we have found all the costumes and props, the characters now know their places, we are ready to start our program with this prayer:

O holy child of Bethlehem, descend to us we pray;
cast out our sin and enter in, be born in us today.
O come to us, abide with us, our Lord Emmanuel.
Amen.

Narrator A: And it came to pass, that Miss Direction's *misplaced Christmas* is actually our program.

Narrator B   Thank you for coming. Let us stand as we sing our closing Christmas carol, "*O Little Town of Bethlehem*. After the song the pastor will come and give the benediction.